Caligula's Nemi Ships: The History of the Roman Emperor's Mysterious Luxury Boats

By Charles River Editors

A Picture of the Remains of One of the Ships

About Charles River Editors

Charles River Editors provides superior editing and original writing services across the digital publishing industry, with the expertise to create digital content for publishers across a vast range of subject matter. In addition to providing original digital content for third party publishers, we also republish civilization's greatest literary works, bringing them to new generations of readers via ebooks.

Sign up here to receive updates about free books as we publish them, and visit Our Kindle Author Page to browse today's free promotions and our most recently published Kindle titles.

Introduction

Lake Nemi

The Nemi Ships

For several centuries, fishermen on Lake Nemi in Italy could see ship wreckage on the floor of the lake, and in 1928, under the patronage of Italian dictator Benito Mussolini, one of the most extraordinary archaeological recovery processes was begun to raise from the floor of Lake Nemi, a small volcanic lake in the Alban Hills, some 30 miles south of Rome, two sunken barges that had lain half buried in the silt since the reign of the Roman Emperor Caligula. The recovery of these two vessels was a massive archaeological operation, unique in scope and scale, but also not atypical of the local and international prestige projects which Mussolini used to embellish his popularity, and for which he had become known. Through undertaking projects of this nature, Mussolini sought not only to highlight the splendor of Italian imperial history but also to recreate it, and to guide the Kingdom of Italy, and his own fascist dictatorship, along the road towards recapturing the glory days of the great Roman Empire.

The recovery of the Nemi Ships was one such enterprise. It presented Mussolini with the opportunity to reveal to the world once again the superiority of ancient Roman culture and technology, while at the same time illustrating the advances in modern Italian technology that allowed for such a daring and groundbreaking salvage operation to take place. As the waters of Lake Nemi subsided, and as the carcasses of the first ship came into view, the shores of the lake were crowded with archaeologists, researchers, journalists and politicians bearing witness to one of the greatest moments in archaeological history.

As it turned out, the two ships dated back to Caligula, with the smaller boat serving as a floating temple and the bigger one serving as a floating palace for Caligula himself. The bigger boat was one of the largest ships ever constructed during antiquity, and it had used technology that would not again be available until the 19th century. For example, in addition to their size, the ships on Lake Nemi used advanced water pumps and anchors, as well as the first evidence of the Romans' use of ball bearings, used to create a platform for a rotating statue.

The ships at Nemi were perfect symbols for the excesses of Caligula, so after Caligula was assassinated, the ships were intentionally scuttled. Unfortunately, that was not the last time the ships met an untimely fate, because in May 1944, during World War II, the Allies were pushing the Nazis north through Italy and a battle was waged in the area. On the night of May 31, the ships were almost completely destroyed in a fire. Both sides blamed the other, but despite their loss, a lot of work has gone into replicating the ships and continuing to display the artifacts that were aboard.

Caligula's Nemi Ships: The History of the Roman Emperor's Mysterious Luxury Barges chronicles the history, discovery, and destruction of the famous ships. Along with pictures of important people, places, and events, you will learn about the Nemi ships like never before, in no time at all.

Caligula's Nemi Ships: The History of the Roman Emperor's Mysterious Luxury Boats
About Charles River Editors
Introduction
   Chapter 1: Caligula
   Chapter 2: Origins of the Ships
   Chapter 3: The Construction of the Ships
   Chapter 4: Artifacts
   Chapter 5: The Salvage Operation
   Chapter 6: The Destruction of the Ships
   Chapter 7: Project Diana
   Online Resources
   Bibliography

Chapter 1: Caligula

The story of the Nemi Ships begins with Emperor Caligula himself; the third emperor of Rome. What is known about Caligula is largely what was written in 121 AD in the only definitive biography of Caligula, his predecessors and successors, *De vita Caesarum* or *About the Life of the Caesars*, more commonly known as *The Twelve Caesars*. This is a biographical study of the Roman general Julius Caesar and the first eleven emperors of Rome, written by Roman historian Gaius Suetonius Tranquillus.[1] As a consequence of this, and much later historical speculation, Caligula has come to be one of the most reviled and enigmatic personalities of the Roman imperial pantheon. He has been painted as the mad emperor, emotionally unstable from birth, corrupted by the agency of an evil and conniving grandfather, and his mental equilibrium tipped over the edge by the inheritance of almost unlimited power. There is, without doubt, an element of truth in all of this, but historians in recent years have sought to challenge this stereotype, pointing instead to the political reforms and public works projects that also characterized the short reign of this most famous of Roman emperors.

---

[1] **Note**: Julius Caesar was not among the Emperors of Rome. It was his ambition to do so that brought about his death, and it was the events that followed his death that began the dynastic process of Roman imperial development.

Bust of Caligular, by Ny Carlsberg Glypyotek

The basic facts of Caligula's life and reign, however, are this: he was born on 31 August AD 12, and died on 24 January AD 41, and is referred to by Suetonius as *Gaius*, alluding to his correct name, which was *Gaius Julius Caesar*. This is not to be confused with his more famous forbear, *Julius Caesar*, although Caligula was, of course, a member of the house of rulers conventionally known as the Julio-Claudian dynasty. The name Caligula was, in fact, simply a nickname given to him by the troops of his father, the great Roman general Germanicus (24 May 15 BC – 10 October AD 19), who was arguably one of the greatest and most successful commanders and military tacticians of his time, and also a member of the same dynasty.

This nickname refers to the word *Caliga*, or a heavy-soled and hobnailed military boot that was typically worn by Roman legionary soldiers and auxiliaries throughout the periods of both the Roman Republic and the Empire. On his journeys with his father through the northern European campaign theatres, Caligula wore a diminutive military uniform, and commanded troops in mock battles and displays staged for his amusement by the apparently adoring legions. The implications of this are that Caligula was known as *Little Boots*, or *Bootikins,* as some less charitable historians have jibed, a name that did not please him greatly during his adulthood, and certainly not during his reign.

Caligula's lineage and access to the throne follows the typically arcane and treacherous route of intrigue and maneuver that began on the *Ides of March* of 44 BC. He was the son of Germanicus, who was the nephew and adopted son of the Emperor Tiberius. Germanicus was one of the most prodigious generals and military personalities of the period who enjoyed great popularity within the army. This, following the trend set by Julius Caesar, positioned him well to ascend to the imperial throne upon the death of the Emperor Tiberius, a death that Germanicus might be tempted to facilitate sooner than nature might have intended. The Emperor, however, acted first, and an agent of Tiberius poisoned Germanicus, according at least to some historic sources, after which the aging emperor kept a very close eye on his wife and sons.

***The Death of Germanicus,* by Nicholas Poussin**

Caligula's youth and adolescence, therefore, was lived very much under the shadow of an aging emperor whose growing paranoia was matched only by his unrestrained power and personal corruption.[2] With the death of his two brothers, attributed in both cases to the indirect actions of Tiberius, Caligula found himself in the very uncomfortable position of being the lone surviving heir of an increasingly cruel and unstable emperor. However, Tiberius, it appears, developed an affection for the young Caligula, and began to groom him for the eventual inheritance of power.

---

[2] **Notes:** Sources vary as to the true legacy of Tiberius. There can be no doubt that his later years were characterized by paranoia, instability and corruption, but he nonetheless was a more prudent ruler than has been popularly suggested, relying more on diplomacy and influence than on military conquest, and he left the Roman treasury in a significantly healthier position than he found it.

Bust of Tiberius

   Tiberius had by then retreated from Rome to the island of Capri, and for six years, Caligula remained under his tutelage. Again, accounts vary as to the nature of his political education, but in general, it can be assumed that he was exposed to the Machiavellian methodologies that Tiberius had by then perfected, along with almost daily exposure to the cruelty and sexual deviancy for which his grandfather had also become notorious. Bearing in mind also the fact that Tiberius had been responsible, at least indirectly, for the death of his father and two brothers, and the exile and impoverishment of his mother, it must have taken a great deal of forbearance and self-control for the young Caligula to remain civil and responsive long enough to survive. According to Suetonius at least, he must have been an extraordinary actor to maintain this façade, assuming that it was a façade, in order eventually to gain ascension to the imperial throne.

   This he did, however, and in 35 AD, he was named heir to the estate of Tiberius. This, by then, was a vast estate indeed, in terms both of Tiberius's personal wealth and the wealth of the Empire. Fiscal prudence had probably been Tiberius's most valuable, if not his most colorful attribute. Caligula, therefore, at the age of 24, suddenly found himself in a position of almost unimaginable power, and with access to an apparently limitless reserve of wealth, and it was this fact, most tend to agree, that very quickly corrupted Caligula, and began to tamper with his sanity and reason.

Suetonius's account of Caligula's life suggests that at least the first year of his reign was moderate and intelligent. Initially he was revered as the son of Germanicus, and perhaps too because he was anyone other than Tiberius. In general, therefore, his ascension to the throne was positively received throughout the empire. In 37 AD, however, he fell seriously ill, perhaps as a consequence of being poisoned, and the experience appears to have triggered a shift in both mood and emphasis. The character of his reign then darkened; he grew paranoid, cruel and self-serving, and many of the more negative associations attributed to his personality owe their origins to this period.

Caligula Depositing the Ashes of His Mother and Brother in the Tomb of His Ancestors, by **Eustache Le Sueur**

According to various historic accounts, Caligula was manifestly insane, self-absorbed, sexually deviant, homicidal and fiscally imprudent. If one was to judge him according to the norms of his age, however, then arguably none of the above would seem particularly incongruent. The inevitability of power corruption, and Caligula's moral descent, are hardly unprecedented, either then, or now. Quite possibly many of his most famous excesses – incest, murder, self-deification, military folly and grandiose self-delusion – were political embellishments based on some historic fact, but with their roots fundamentally in the popular response to his poor governance and fiscal irresponsibility.

Nevertheless, in January 41 AD, Caligula was assassinated by his own Praetorian Guard, bringing to an end one of the most controversial episodes of Roman imperial history. His legacy has since remained saturated by his extravagances, and no doubt he will remain symbolic of Roman imperial excess, but it should not be forgotten that he was also responsible for considerable innovation, and a great deal of Roman civic improvement.

Arguably, one of the greatest of these contributions were improvements to the harbors at Rhegium and Sicily, both of which facilitated increased grain imports from Egypt, and a lowering of food prices. He also completed the construction of the temple of Augustus and the theatre of Pompey, and began work on an amphitheatre beside the Saepta. Likewise, he ordered the construction of the two aqueducts, the *Aqua Claudia* and *Anio Novus*, both, for the time, little less than engineering marvels. Moreover, he initiated the construction of a large racetrack known as the circus of *Gaius* and *Nero*, and had an Egyptian obelisk, now known as the *Vatican Obelisk*, transported by sea and erected in the centre of Rome. In addition, he had new roads built and instituted polices to retain and improve the existing network of Roman roads. Bearing in mind that he sat on the throne for just three years and ten months, these were no small achievements. However, more notable have always been the grandiose follies and monumental expressions of power and immortality for which he was better known.

In 39 AD, for example, Caligula ordered the construction of a temporary pontoon bridge, using Roman naval ships as the pontoons, stretching over the Bay of Naples between the resort of Baiae and the neighboring port of Puteoli. Over this bridge, Caligula rode his horse, wearing the armored breastplate of Alexander the Great. This illogical enterprise was in part a petulant response to a prediction made by Tiberius's soothsayer, and in part to rival the Persian king Xerxes's crossing of the Hellespont.[3]

At other times, Caligula declared war on Neptune, leading his troops into the waves to strike at the heart of the Roman God of the Seas. Sensitive about his premature baldness, he declared it a capital crime for anyone to look down at him from above as he passed by, frequently ordering those with a fine head of hair to be shaved. Subject to bisexual and incestuous promiscuities, he eventually impregnated his sister Drusilla, whom he then disemboweled to remove the unborn and would-be demigod child from the womb. Upon Drusilla's death Caligula had her deified.

However, arguably Caligula's most grandiose and self-serving folly, which was also his most brilliant project, was ordering the construction of two floating pleasure palaces on Lake Nemi, an undertaking that challenged not only the Roman fiscus, but also the nautical engineering prowess

---

[3] **Note:** Thrasyllus of Mendes stated that Caligula had *'no more chance of becoming emperor than of riding a horse across the Bay of Baiae'*

of contemporary Roman shipbuilders.

Chapter 2: Origins of the Ships

The transportation of the Vatican Obelisk from Egypt to Rome had required the construction of a specific ship, or barge, which became the first of Caligula's naval engineering projects on a significant scale. Known as Caligula's *Giant Ship*, it had a length of between 95 and 104 meters (341 ft), and a beam of about 20.3 m (66 ft), and displaced a minimum of 7400 tons. Having completed the task of transporting the monument, the ship was scuttled in order to create an artificial mole enclosing an anchorage in the port of Ostia, which then became the foundation of a large lighthouse. This lighthouse, incidentally, was an imitation of the famous lighthouse in Alexandria, the *Pharos of Alexandria*. The remains of this ship were unearthed during the construction of the Leonardo da Vinci Airport outside Rome, and some parts of it remain preserved in a museum housing the remains of several smaller vessels also unearthed at the same site.

The two ships recovered from Lake Nemi, however, were each over a hundred feet shorter in length than the Giant Ship, and so did not represent any particular precedent in engineering for the times. The principal challenge seems to have been building the ships in-situ, and equipping them for the conditions of relatively shallow water. It would perhaps be fair to say that the Giant Ship represented a far greater engineering feat, since it was designed and constructed for a practical maritime purpose, and the fact that the *Vatican Obelisk* currently sits where it does is proof of its efficiency. The Nemi ships, however, had a more obscure purpose, and since they were built on inland water without navigational potential, and were for the most part stationary, it is inevitable that they served either a ceremonial purpose, or were a project of personal aggrandizement, probably both.

Before we dwell in any particular detail on the construction of the ships, however, let us examine the possible motivation for their construction. It must be added here that almost no period literature exists to shed any light on the matter, and in fact, the ships were never attributed to Caligula until his proprietary mark was discovered on lead piping in 1931, after the ships were raised. Therefore, historians and archaeologists have had to rely on contemporary records and the interpretation of artifacts to try to decode the mystery of the Nemi Ships.

The appointments of both vessels initially suggest that each was intended as luxury pleasure craft, and an embellishment of Caligula's status and reputation. In this regard, it has been noted that Caligula both admired, and attempted to exceed, the accomplishments and luxuries of the Hellenistic/Ptolemaic dynasties of Egypt, Sicily and Syracuse, and that this might have been his primary motivation.[4] However, a snippet of history provided by Pliny the Younger suggests that

---

[4] **Note:** The Ptolemaic Kingdom was an ancient Greek, or Hellenistic kingdom that was based in Egypt and ruled by the Ptolemaic dynasty, which began with Ptolemy I Soter's accession after the death of Alexander the Great in 323 BC, and which ended with the death of Cleopatra VII and the Roman conquest in 30 BC.

since Lake Nemi was sacred (it was home to the cult of the Goddess Diana), Roman law prohibited ships from sailing on it, as a consequence of which, Caligula would have to have received a religious exemption for his ships.[5] In compliance with this, therefore, some ritual or religious/symbolic significance would have been necessary.

In this regard, it is worth noting that the Nemi Lake was also commonly referred to as *Speculum Dianae* or *The Mirror of Diana*, because, from the surrounding hills, it reflected the full moon, which also reflected off the distant Tyrrhenian Sea. This was in reference to the Goddess Diana, in part goddess of the moon, or Diana *Nemorensis* (loosely translated as "woodsy" Diana), who Caligula is reported to have revered and venerated.[6] The Temple of Diana, the centre of the cult, was located in a grove of oak trees on the north shore of Lake Nemi, and architectural iconography referring to Diana is still visible in many places. At the full moon, when the cult was active, Caligula could frequently be found at Nemi, appealing to the woods and the lake for the goddess to appear before him. In all likelihood, therefore, he dedicated one, or both of the ships to Diana, but possibly also to Isis, or any other of the many deities relevant at that time.

At a certain point, however, both ships, stripped of their valuables, were intentionally scuttled, thereafter coming to rest in intact condition in the soft clay of the lakebed. In an environment without significant currents they rested, surviving in a state of almost complete preservation until they were discovered and raised, after which they offered a unique opportunity for marine archaeology to study Roman maritime construction techniques and naval architecture.

Chapter 3: The Construction of the Ships

Like the British Empire, the Roman Empire before it was built on the power and reach of naval and merchant shipping, and the extraordinary number of ancient Roman wrecks that have been, and still are being uncovered around the Mediterranean, and the west coast of Europe, hint at the sheer volume of regional shipping underway during that period. Roman ship construction, therefore, was a massive industry, perhaps the only real industry of the period. Methods and techniques had been inherited largely from the Greeks, and the Egyptians before that, but the organization, the scale and the logistical capabilities were purely Roman.

The fundamental element of ancient shipbuilding in general, but Roman shipbuilding in particular, was the use of what was known as the *shell-first* technique. The Roman system of shell-first construction was known as the *Vitruvian method*, codified by the Roman architect and engineer Marcus Vitruvius Pollio (born c. 80–70 BC, died after c. 15 BC), who was perhaps best known for his multi-volume work entitled *De Architectura*. Typically, the outer hull of a ship was fashioned from oak planking, only after which was the internal rib structure installed. This is

---

[5] **Note:** Gaius Plinius Caecilius Secundus, born Gaius Caecilius or Gaius Caecilius Cilo (61 AD –113 AD), better known as *Pliny the Younger* was a lawyer, author, and magistrate of Ancient Rome.

[6] **Note:** Diana was the Roman goddess of the hunt, the moon and childbirth, associated with wild animals and woodland, and having the power to talk and communicate to and control animals. She was conflated with the Greek goddess Artemis, though in Italy she had an independent origin. Revered in Roman Neopaganism and Stregheria, Diana was worshipped as the virgin goddess of childbirth and women. She was one of the three maiden goddesses, Diana, Minerva and Vesta, who swore never to marry.

the reverse of more modern techniques, which establish the structure and shape of the ship through an internal system of ribs, upon which are then clad the materials used in the construction of the hull. Most of the strength, therefore, would be inherent in the planking itself, and not to quite the same extent the beams and internal structure. These were inserted in order to maintain form and structural coherence, but not as a defined framework upon which the structure of the vessel could be pinned.

A Drawing of Vitruvius (right)

Early Mediterranean shipbuilding techniques deployed a system of ligatures, or lashings, to join and secure the planking, typically in combination with treenails, with the later mortise and tenon system either superseding, or overlapping this technique. Typically, a single keel was set, upon which planking was fashioned, utilizing edge joining either through ligature or mortise and tenon, most often with a single layer of planking, but quite often with a double layer of laminated planking with a protective layer in between.

This method is still visible today in traditional boat manufacturing in many parts of the world, perhaps most notably in the construction of small coastal dhows in East Africa and on the various Indian Ocean islands. The formality of naval and merchant ship construction in the Mediterranean theatre, however, created a system of standardized manufacturing techniques, which were similar to, but an evolution of earlier techniques, based on considerable technical advances.

The standardization of manufacturing and the establishment of a centralized industry began in

27 BC, when Marcus Agrippa, the principal aide-de-camp at the time of Emperor Augustus, established a naval base in Misenum, on the north shore of the Bay of Naples. Here were established the shipyards that would support the massive naval construction programs that would in turn sustain the imperial expansions under Augustus and Tiberius. Throughout this period, there were significant military/territorial advances made, in particular in Egypt and Europe, all of which demanded an enormous output of naval transport and war tonnage. Likewise, as the empire expanded, and as trade networks followed, and at times preceded military advance, Roman maritime architecture became a virtual industry unto itself.

It was some time in 39 AD that Caligula, having disposed of his quixotic project to build and ride across a pontoon bridge spanning the Bay of Naples, ordered the construction of the two Nemi ships. He had by then already completed the construction of a private villa on the shores of the lake, and had by then begun to display the first signs of his signature erratic, personal behavior and undisciplined and extravagant spending. He summoned a group of naval architects and engineers to his villa, and ordered them to submit designs for the construction of two huge vessels based on Caligula's own specifications.

The naval architects, however, appeared to have been responsible only for the construction of the hulls and the basic platform. When the ships were later raised, studied and mapped, it quickly became clear that there had been a lack of coordination between the design and construction of the hulls and that of the superstructure. This suggested that once built and floated, responsibility passed from the hands of naval shipbuilders to civil architects, engineers, artists, artisans and builders to complete the internal appointments, and to adorn the ships with many of their practical and decorative features.

Bearing in mind that both ships were built in situ, one can but marvel at the sheer weight of the undertaking, and the technical mastery that was required to pull off an operation on this scale. Such a mobilization of resources was one that only the army and navy would have been able to practically mount, and it is clear from the construction techniques that those responsible for building the ships were indeed using the standard shipbuilding techniques of the period that were typically applied to naval vessels. For example, both ships were clad in three layers of lead, a standard preservation procedure intended to prevent infestations of shipworms, which would not have been necessary in fresh water, and so this was quite clearly an unnecessary and expensive addition. This once again clearly indicates the monolithic dimensions of Roman engineering capability, and likewise hints at the scale and standardization of procedures that, in nature of large organizations, were unable to adapt to the specific needs of individual projects.

A similar example was that both ships were equipped with steering mechanisms, although only the temple ship, or *seconda nave* (the second ship recovered during salvage, although it was the larger of the two), was powered by oars, indicated by the fact that it had been designed with benches and outriggers sufficient to support up to one hundred oarsmen. On a body of water 0.64 square miles in area, within which neither ship could effectively maneuver, the presence of over 100 oarsmen would seem superficial to say the least. In all probability, the ships were anchored in position, and there they remained as a static fixture.

The chief technical difficulty, however, was not the massive size of the two ships – Roman shipbuilders, as we have seen, were capable of building big – but the shallow draft necessary to float such large ships on the relatively small crater lake. Typically, the first phase of construction of a ship would have been to set the keel, followed by establishing the profile. In this case, however the first phase was probably the construction of the profile, followed by the laying of the keel, which in the case of the palace ship was in fact five keels, necessary to facilitate the wide berth but low draft. This would have required the naval architects charged with designing and constructing this ship to conceptualize it as five separate ships combined into one.

The next phase was the construction of the shell up to the third wale, above the gunwale, or the topgallant bulwarks, which were in effect bulwarks fitted above the rail to afford additional shelter on deck. Thereafter the ribs were inserted and secured with iron nails bent, or double bent, possibly electro-coated with copper, or with copper applied during the smelting process. Tens of thousands of these nails were recovered from the wreck, and were in such a remarkable state of preservation that is seems unlikely that one or other procedure was not applied. Both ships comprised two decks, an upper and a lower deck, and some 140 oak frames.

Then the hull was triple coated in lead, with the upper or topside timbers, primarily comprising cedar, were protected using paint and tarred wool. Both ships were equipped with 11.3 meter (37 ft) quarter oars, with the *seconda nave* equipped with four of these – two off each quarter and two from the shoulder, while the *prima nave* was equipped with only two. Oars ostensibly powered the *seconda nave*, but the *prima nave* had no visible means of propulsion, so it was either anchored or stationary, or towed into position when in use.

Ultimately, the *prima nave* was found to be 70 meters (230 ft) long with a beam (width) of 20 meters (66 ft). Uniquely configured for the period, the shape of the hull appears wider at the stern and narrower at the bow, and divided into three sections, with the main section displaced towards the rear of the ship. It contained at least one large building and several smaller, associated buildings with numerous antechambers and interlinking corridors. This was the pleasure palace, with central heating, extravagant fixtures, gilded copper roof tiles and mosaic floors.

The *seconda nave*, the larger of the two ships at 73 meters (240 ft) was the temple ship. This was the better preserved of the two, and so was easier to reconstruct and interpret. The superstructure appears to have been built with a main section amidships, a heavy building at the rear and a smaller one at the prow, connected by sheltered colonnades with an internal courtyard. Although little remained at salvage of either of these buildings, their presence was indicated by a shorter spacing of the deck-supporting crossbeams where the two heavy structures had stood, and the distribution of ballast to compensate for uneven weight topside. The outriggers and benches for the oarsmen were probably never used.

Chapter 4: Artifacts

Once the basic construction of the ships had been completed, the project was taken over by civil architects, artists, craftsmen and engineers. Caligula's objective was not merely to emulate the Ptolemaic kings, but to supersede them, and so of critical importance to him were the appointments. As a ferment of hostile feeling was beginning to boil in Rome against the extravagance and financial irresponsibility of the young Emperor, Caligula installed himself on the shores of Lake Nemi and oversaw the most profligate and expensive aspect of the project. Both ships were designed to satisfy his appetite for luxury and indulgence, with perhaps a superficial association with the Cult of Diana.[7] The cult of Diana contained aspects of violence, human sacrifice and ritual sex, all of which were likely to have appealed to the darker side of Caligula's nature, and provided the edification and on board entertainment. Both ships, however, in particular the *prima nave*, the palace ship, were richly appointed, and really were nothing less than palatial houseboats for the pleasure of Caligula himself and his entourage.

While the technologies used in the basic construction of the ship were impressive enough, arguably the more interesting and innovative technologies were those applied in the building and embellishment of the superstructure. The palace ship was conceived and built as a pleasure palace, and as such was adorned with some of the most beautiful and original architectural embellishments and modern luxuries of the age. Early salvage efforts at the site during the European Middle Ages unearthed a few objects and artifacts that were of such extraordinarily fine artistry and manufacture that it was clear to those curious about the many rumors that there was indeed something large and extremely lucrative nestled in the mud of Lake Nemi.

Probably the most recognizable and iconic of these artifacts are the bronze animal head moorings that decorated the heads of the beams, and were used as mooring for the many lighters and smaller craft that would have serviced the palace ship, and ferried passengers back and forth. These had the additional ritualistic function of keeping evil at bay. Likewise, a number of clay pipes were brought to the surface during salvage, and these proved to be part of a *hypocaust*, or an elaborate under-floor heating system.

The word *hypocaust* derives from the Ancient Greek *hypo* meaning under, and *caust*, meaning burn. Typically, the floor was raised above the ground by pillars, called *pilae* stacks, which were usually just columns of stacked ceramic tiles, with a layer of tiles above, followed by a layer of concrete before a second layer of tiles or mosaic on the upper side. Spaces inside the walls allowed hot air and smoke from the furnace to circulate before being expelled through flues in the roof, which heated the walls, thus heating the room without fouling the interior with smoke.

This system was both elaborate and expensive, and so typically reserved for public baths, or the villas of extremely wealthy individuals. The system aboard the Nemi ships, however, was the first recorded incident of hypocaust construction in relation to maritime architecture, and it was a particularly fine example. The typical construction of a hypocaust made use of pillars built from stacked ceramic tiles. The Nemi ship, however, utilized a system of ceramic tubes or cylinders, which would appear to be a considerably more sophisticated and expensive system, although utilizing the same principal. No evidence remains of wall heating, although one can suppose that it would have been included, and scant evidence remains of what would have been the lavish

---

[7] **Note:** Caligula's interest in the Hellenistic/Egyptian dynasties prompted an interest in the Isis cult, not dissimilar to the Cult of Diana, and certain surviving decorative features reflect the possibility that the dedication of the vessels was to Isis, and not to Diana.

mosaic floors warmed by this system, which probably combined a Roman bath.

An associated technology was the system of lead pipes that facilitated the internal plumbing system, regulated by finely crafted bronze faucets, or taps. Only one of these taps was recovered during salvation, and initially it was thought to be far too well preserved and too technologically advanced for it to be associated with a Roman era wreck. However, it was easily matched to the on-board water system, revealing, once again, a far greater Roman mastery of foundry and metal casting techniques than had previously been understood. This bronze tap is strikingly similar in structure to modern systems of taps and water flow regulation, with a slightly tapering and perforated pin resting in a conical barrel and connecting in-line two lead pipes. The manufacture of this item, similar in every respect to taps still being manufactured in the region today, was so precise that it still maintains a watertight seal today, indicating once again that even down to these mundane fixtures, the best of Roman engineering was brought to bear on this project.

And there were more surprises in store. Found among the mass of debris associated with the wrecks was what would prove to be one of the earliest working examples of rolling-element ball and roller bearings. After a great deal of study and speculation, it was concluded that these had been used to facilitate the rotation of a statue or monument, possibly that of Diana, which was achieved by a turntable using what was in practical terms an early system of thrust bearing.

What appeared to have been achieved was a moving pair of turntables upon one another, with the statue on the uppermost revolving on a bearing system arranged in a circle. In one example, the bearings took the form of eight bronze balls, each having a pair of trunnions, and each securely fitted into journals in the upper turntable. The other example comprised wheels made up of up to eight tapered or conical wooden rollers, similarly journaled. It would be incorrect to describe these as true roller or ball bearings insofar as the latter tend to move independently within a casing, or circular groove called a race, with neither trunnions nor journal bearings. Nonetheless, this was the earliest known manifestation of a roller or ball bearing system, predating previous experimentations made by Leonardo da Vinci and his peers by several centuries.

Divers brought the first of these curious spherical bronze balls to the surface in 1895, sixteen of which are now preserved in the *Museo Nazionale Romano*. It was not until the 1830s, however, when many more loose balls were retrieved, including two secured by iron straps to a fragment of wood that archaeologists began to suspect what they might represent. In 1940, Italian engineer Guido Ucelli, the man commissioned by Benito Mussolini to undertake the final salvage operation, published a book entitled *Le Navi di Nemi*, which is now recognized as the definitive tract on the salvage operation, and the artifacts discovered. Ucelli, as an engineer, was most interested in the discovery of these curious bronze balls, some of which showed clear signs of having been machined by some sort of a turning method. A number of cylindrical bronze rollers were later found, although their purpose remains a mystery. A third and most remarkable find, however, perhaps associated with the same on-board function, was a number of trunnion-mounted wooden rollers within wooden rings. Ucelli put forward the opinion that these represented an early taper-roller thrust bearing system. Initially the explanation for these various bearings was that they were part of a mechanism to bring up the anchor, or some other mechanical function of the ship, but archeologists ultimately concluded that they simply allowed a platform supporting the statute of a goddess to be turned by a crank system from below deck.

Yet another unexpected and startling discovery was a five-meter-long lead-stock anchor of a pattern thought only to be in regular use during the early Medieval period, and similar to the pattern known as the *British Admiralty Anchor*. This was one of three anchors to ultimately be recovered, which in combination shed a great deal of new light on the types of anchors in use aboard Roman naval vessels at the beginning of the Christian era. The anchor was made of wood, but was fitted with a heavy lead stock.[8] This confirmed that the numerous lead bars with square holes in them that had been found at various wreck sites across the Mediterranean were not simple weighted anchors themselves, as had previously been thought, but anchor stocks. The wooden anchor was found in a correct holding attitude, with one arm dug in and the stock parallel to the ground. The wood and lead anchor was lighter than the iron anchor, and lighter than those typically used on ocean going shipping – more in keeping, in fact, with anchors used regularly by vessels confined, for example, to the lower reaches of the Nile and the Nile Delta.

The second anchor discovered was made of iron, and sheathed in wood. The wood gave the iron core a larger bearing surface, which certainly was an advantage in thick mud found at the bottom of Lake Nemi. The extra area of the shank and arms prevented the anchor from sinking too far into the mud. It featured an 18 ft. (5.4 meters) oak shank with two oak, iron-tipped arms and a 7 ft. 10 in. (2 meter) solid lead stock. The discovery of this anchor explained the presence of lead bars found about the shores of the Mediterranean that weighed up to 1380 pounds.

The third was an all-iron common anchor weighing 900 pounds, its shank 11 ft. 8in. (3.5 meters) long, and its stock 9 ft. 9 in. (3 meters) long. The stock was held in place by a cotter pin, and so stowing was easily accomplished by removing the pin and the stock and laying the anchor flat.

Other, perhaps more mundane technologies were also unearthed. Elements of two finely crafted bronze chain-and-bucket bilge pumps, for example, were found; one associated with each ship. These comprised a simple waterwheel system, but with their elements beautifully crafted and expertly designed. At the top of each, a drum was mounted on a horizontal shaft over which the chain of buckets passed. At each end of this shaft was a wooden flywheel with a crank handle.[9] Part of the significance of these two pumps is that they were one of the first recorded incidences of the use of a crank system outside of simple hand-mills and querns.[10] Cranks increasingly appear in the archaeological record from about 1 AD onwards, thereafter becoming established technology during the early medieval period.

A second, hand operated twin cylinder piston pump was also discovered and reconstructed, and this, again for its times, was extremely sophisticated and technically advanced. Although there

---

[8] An anchor stock is the cross spar located at the top of the shank, just below the coupling.

[9] **Note:** Such a flywheel was found, but it has never been incontrovertibly ascertained whether this was in fact part of the pump.

[10] **Note:** Quern-stones are stone tools for hand-grinding a wide variety of materials. They were used in pairs. The lower, stationary, stone is called a quern, while the upper mobile stone is called a hand stone. They were first used in the Neolithic to grind cereals into flour.

would no doubt have been more than one of these, only one was found. The recovered example functioned as a double acting, double cylinder force pump that lifted water from a rainwater tank below deck on the upstroke, and on the down stroke forced it through a system of lead pipes to a second tank, or reservoir at the back of the ship, where it was pressurized and then distributed around the ship.

These, along with the tap described above, where linked into a plumbing system facilitated by a number of lead pipes, and it was the examination of these pipes that solved perhaps the greatest mystery of the Nemi ships. Stamped into a number of these were the words: C. CAESARIS AVG. GERMANIC, meaning, the property of Gaius Caesar Augustus Germanicus. It was now clear who had owned these behemoths, and who it was that had ordered their construction.

Chapter 5: The Salvage Operation

A year after the completion and launch of the Nemi Ships, Caligula was assassinated, whereupon they were stripped and scuttled, and for centuries they lay forgotten, slowly subsiding into the mud of Lake Nemi.[11] The legend of the Nemi ships, however, persisted, and while memories of the original ownership and function of the vessels faded, and then disappeared altogether, the knowledge of their existence did not. During periods of drought and low water, the upper timbers of the wrecks could sometimes be seen from the bluffs overlooking the lake. Rumors of great treasure sustained interest, and across the centuries a number of efforts were made to reach the wrecks.

Both ships lay on a sloping bank, but the *seconda nave*, the palace ship, lay closer to the shore, and so in shallower water, and was consequently more visible, and generally more easily accessible. A trickle of artifacts, typically amphorae, appeared in the hands of collectors, as well as sections of timber and occasional architectural fixtures, as villagers and local fishermen used grappling hooks and anchors to tear at the wrecks. The first formal attempt at salvage took place in 1446, when Leon Battista Alberti, an Italian polymath in the da Vinci tradition, became interested in the legend of the ships. Alberti was a humanist author, artist, architect, poet, priest, linguist, philosopher and cryptographer, and was supported in his efforts to salvage the wrecks by a non-conformist and influential local prelate, Cardinal Prospero Colonna.

---

[11] This dating of the ship's scuttling is speculative. It has been assumed that the event was associated with the assassination of Caligula, but coins found amongst artifacts recovered from the wreck suggest that at least one ship was still in use during the reign of the emperor Nero. Nero, however, was no less unpopular than Caligula, and shared similar proclivities, suggesting that upon his declaration by the senate to be a public enemy, and his suicide, the ships may have been destroyed.

Leon Battista Alberti

Such salvage operations stretched the ingenuity and imagination of fifteenth century engineers, leading to several attempts to design and construct primitive diving suits using tar lined boxes and glass fascia as primitive underwater masks, combined with various types of breathing apparatus as well as inflatable bladders to raise and lower divers. Alberti succeeded in raising part of the hull using a team of divers from Genoa. However, this early effort achieved little more than to damage the wrecks, pulling off timbers and stripping off much of the remaining superstructure and scattering artifacts. All that could be established from these efforts was the type of timbers used, and the fact that the ships had been clad in lead. Much of interest and value, however, continued to come to the surface over the years, certainly enough to fuel ongoing rumors that a treasure trove of artifacts lay waiting to be discovered below the waters of Nemi.

The next coordinated and recorded attempt came a century later when Italian Francesco De Marchi made a diving expedition to the wreck using an early diving bell and a wooden dive helmet. His discoveries included bricks, marble paving stones, bronze, copper, lead artifacts and quantities of timber beams. The latter were turned into walking sticks and other items for sale to tourists and local nobility who regularly visited the site of his work. This had been the most comprehensive and successful salvage effort so far, but its academic underpinnings were slim, and in general De Marchi was interested less in advancing knowledge than profiting from the artifacts, and so most of what he has brought to the surface was not catalogued and recorded, but sold, and so has since been lost.

The next significant attempt to explore the wrecks would not take place for a further three centuries, at which point a rather quixotic Italian by the name of Annesio Fusconi built a floating platform from which to raise the wrecks using a complex system of cables and pulleys. These cables, however, proved not to be strong enough, and so Fusconi abandoned the site and went off in search of alternatives. Upon returning, he discovered that local farmers had dismantled his platforms to make wine and oil barrels, and the project was abandoned.

In the meanwhile, in 1885, the British Ambassador to Italy, Sir John Savile Lumley, or Lord Savile as he would later become, found himself interested in the piecemeal archaeological work underway in Nemi, and began his own excavations as an amateur archaeologist. With a purchased license, and the permission of the landowner, Prince Beroaldo Orsini, he began to sink exploratory trenches with the objective of locating and excavating the original site of the Temple of Diana.

Saville was arguably the first individual with the right combination of resources, time and academic interest to begin treating the area around Lake Nemi with the kind of academic respect that it was due, and he was not disappointed. At the foot of the hill on which the town of Nemi now stands, he unearthed the remains of a large wall, previously buried beneath dense vegetation, that he guessed was part of the original temple of Diana. The wall appeared to support the banks above it, whilst at the same time forming the north and east sides of what was later revealed to be a vast terrace measuring in excess of 44,000 m2, or over 450,000 ft2. There Lord Savile immediately set to work, and from his very first trench, he unearthed a cornucopia of terracotta models and statuettes, presumably offerings to the Goddess Diana, and the presence of numerous statuettes of the Goddess herself that strongly supported his premise that this was indeed the lost temple of Diana.

Ultimately, an enormous haul of artifacts was recovered, and a series of small chapels and shrines revealed beneath the original north wall. Among the artifacts were countless terracotta fragments, the head of a horse, an imposing sculpture of Tiberius and a beautiful and unusually well-preserved statue of a Roman matron, named *Fundilia*. One of the most notable finds, however, towards the end of excavation, was a circular sacrificial altar with channels to drain away blood, surmised to be the temple's external sacrificial altar to Diana.

Consequent to his agreement with the Italian authorities, Lord Savile was permitted to keep only half of the artifacts that he recovered, the balance of which would accrue to the landowner. Prince Orsini, however, in keeping with the European nobility of the time, was financially disadvantaged and so seized on the opportunity to make a significant return on his haul by selling it off to various international art collectors.

Lord Savile, dismayed at this attitude to antiquity, discontinued his work and donated his own collection to the newly established Nottingham Castle Museum and Art Gallery, close to his English ancestral home of Rufford Abbey. The new collection comprised some 1,586 artifacts and an archive of photographic records of the dig.

Lord Savile attempted to establish a code of conduct in relation to the haphazard salvage work hitherto undertaken on the Nemi wrecks, but he was to be ultimately disappointed. Ten years later, in 1895, another salvage operation began, which, although no less acquisitional, was at least somewhat more in keeping with the higher principles of archaeology.

By then the origins of the ships had slipped so far into antiquity that neither myth nor memory recalled any association with Roman history, and certainly not the mad emperor Caligula. The ships were simply a vast enigma, and little more than a rumor. In 1895, however, under the sponsorship of the Italian Ministry of Education, a certain Eliseo Borghi began a relatively competent survey of the wreck site, discovering for the first time that the lakebed contained not one, but two wrecks. Among the artifacts recovered during this survey was the bronze tiller head of one of the rudders, and many of the bronze heads of wild animals that had held in place the mooring rings.

However, recognizing immediately the potential fortune at rest under the waters of Lake Nemi, Borghi suddenly went rogue, placing all of the artifacts that he had unearthed in a private museum, thereafter offering them for sale to the Government, while in the meanwhile continuing furiously, and indiscriminately to loot the wrecks.

An urgent legal application was made by the Department of Antiquities and Fine Arts to halt this recovery, and to place Borghi's collection under state control, and thereafter halt any further desiccation of the site. Soon afterwards, responsibility for investigating the wreck was placed where it should have been, in the hands of the Italian Navy. A naval survey commission, utilizing a team of navy divers, visited the site, and over several weeks subjected it to its first comprehensive analysis and mapping. Ultimately, the report determined that the two ships had settled under some 20 meters or more of water, located 180 meters apart, lying deeply embedded in mud, and under a burden of tons of marble, mosaics, bricks and tile. The only feasible way of raising the wrecks, it was concluded, would be to drain the lake. Such a bold archaeological project would naturally necessitate quantities of qualified engineering expertise and substantial long-term resources, which for the time being were not forthcoming. No plans, therefore, were put forward to salvage the wrecks, and the site was placed for the time being under official protection.

There, once again, matters rested. In the meanwhile, great changes were overtaking Europe as the polarization of fascism and communism on the continent saw the rise of militancy, rearmament and ultra-nationalism. At the vanguard of this movement was Italian dictator Benito Mussolini, who came into power in 1922 on a wave of nationalist revival, a large part of which came in response to his calls for the rediscovery of the pride of Italy, and the glory of her ancient empire. During his period of rule in Italy (31 October 1922 – 25 July 1943), Mussolini sponsored numerous archaeological surveys and excavations, most notably those in Rome, Ostia, Sicily and the Libyan sites of Leptis Magna and Sabratha.[12]

---

[12] **Note:** Italian interest and control in Libya began after the *Italo-Turkish War* of 1911 to 1912, and continued until Italy was defeated by the Allies in the North Africa Campaign of WWII.

Moreover, for Mussolini there was much to be gained by this. Not unlike Caligula, he had a weakness for prestige projects and personal aggrandizement. He was interested in associating the rise of fascist Italy with the magnificence of the Roman Empire, inspiring the masses of the population with a sense of past glory and future destiny. He also hoped, however, that the more thoughtful enterprises of exploring Italy's archaeological heritage would attract to his movement the intellectual middle classes of Italy. It is also perhaps true that his personal fascination with the emperors of Rome reflected a certain interest in becoming one himself, and without doubt, the Nemi ships, at that point only vaguely understood, represented a rare opportunity for him to glimpse into the private lives of the great personalities of the past.

Benito Mussolini

Mussolini certainly entertained the possibility that the new Roman Empire, or the Italian Kingdom as it was then, could once again reclaim some of the old prestige, and old territory of the past. While the Nazis tended to build their ideological foundations on German Aryan ideals, Mussolini went to work on the basis of Italian manifest destiny. He ordered the invasion of Ethiopia as a foothold in North Africa, overwhelming the ancient armies of that region and driving Emperor Haile Selassie into exile. From there he absorbed Somaliland, threatening the British Empire in Africa all the way down to the borders of South Africa. The Italian armed forces took occupation of Libya and much of the Sudan, and in alliance with Hitler, Mussolini allowed himself to picture a recapture of some, if not all of the old Roman provinces of the Mediterranean.

In the meanwhile, he nurtured an ongoing interesting in the gradually broadening picture of the two great ships at rest in the mud of Lake Nemi. If the ships could not be raised, he determined, then, indeed, the level of the lake would be lowered. This was a unique moment in history, he said, "a matter of both science and national pride, a debt of honor to the dignity of our nation."

It could only be at a point, somewhat as it had been in the past, when the whims of a dictator could translate almost immediately into national policy, that such a project could be conceived and undertaken. To achieve this vast ambition, it was decided that an ancient Roman outlet from the lake, an *emissarium*, would be used to channel the water out of the crater, further down towards a second lake, Lake Albanus, and thereafter, via a second emissarium, to the sea.

An emissarium is typically described as an open or subterranean natural or artificial channel by which an outlet is formed or created to carry off water for a variety of reasons. The two *emissarium*, *emissaria* or *emissario* of Lake Albanus and Lake Nemi in the Alban Hills are regarded as being among the most notable examples of such engineering projects, and among the great marvels of ancient Roman engineering.

The Etruscans and early Romans, as history has illustrated, excelled at hydraulic engineering, and no better example of this can be found than the many Roman aqueducts that testify not only to Roman architectural and engineering prowess, but also to Roman civil engineering and surveying techniques, which are also, of course, evident in the extraordinary network of Roman roads.

The emissary of Lake Nemi is another such example. It is about 1600 meters long, more or less a mile, and was constructed sometime during the fifth or sixth century BC as a means of maintaining an even water level during seasonal rainfall, and also to protect the shrine of the Goddess Diana, the earliest structures for which date back more or less to this period. It drained the water of Nemi into Lake Albano, twice as large, and located at a lower elevation, itself also drained by an emissary.

With an east/west orientation, three tunnels were ultimately constructed, the second perhaps to compensate for a collapse of the first, and the third to avoid water infiltration onto the surrounding rock. The tunnels began at the opposing ends of the crater, with ventilation and access shafts being sunk at various points along the way. As further testimony to Roman standards of engineering, the two points of the tunnel met almost exactly, with just a slight adjustment at the junction to compensate for less than a meter of misalignment. A number of channels were dug into the sides of the tunnels that would, presumably, have held sluices to inhibit or direct the flow of water, and perhaps to keep the tunnels free of debris.

It was only in the early 1920s that these tunnels were catalogued and explored, suddenly presenting Mussolini and his antiquities department with a rare and unique opportunity. Roman technologies could be combined in a spectacular public relations exercise on behalf of the great El Duce to illustrate once again the magnificent birthright that the Italian people were heir to. Using the emissarium as a conduit, and modern turbine technology, it would indeed be possible to drain the lake, and expose after almost two thousand years these great and enigmatic ships.

In April 1927, a commission was formed to study the feasibility of salvaging the ships, the expenses likely to be entailed and the probability of success. The tunnels were duly cleared and mapped, and determined to be functional. Five local engineering, electrical and hydraulic firms offered their services to the commission free of charge. On January 3, 1928, signatures were committed to a contract, offers were accepted and work began immediately.

The electrical firm of *Ritta*, Milan, in conjunction with the *Ansaldo Motor Company* and the gas and electric companies of Rome and of Campagna, undertook to supply the necessary equipment for four giant electric pumps that would force water out of the lake and into the emissary. To haul all of the personnel and equipment up to the site, the electrical firm of Stigler constructed a funicular traveling a distance of 270 meters, and carrying a maximum of 40 passengers. The work proceeded in conjunction with the government and archeological authorities, and took a little over four years to complete.

Charged with the responsibility of facilitating and supervising the work was Italian engineer Guido Ucelli, about whom very little is known. Guido Ucelli played a pivotal role, not only in the salvage operation, but also later in recording and publishing the results of the project. His book, *Le Navi di Nemi*, although extremely inaccessible, nonetheless brings together the entirety of information now available on the subject of the Nemi ships, and it is regarded as the definitive work. He was an electrical, hydraulic and mechanical engineer, a banker and businessman, and an early ally of Mussolini. In 1944, he was briefly jailed for providing unspecified assistance in the deportation of Italian Jews. In 1928, he was named promoter and principal executor of the Nemi salvage operation, for which he was later awarded the title *Patron of Nemi*. He died Aug. 23, 1964.

On October 20, 1928, meanwhile, Benito Mussolini arrived on the shore of Lake Nemi, and standing alongside Guido Ucelli, he threw the switch that set the great turbines spinning, heaving volumes of water from the lake and into the nearby emissarium. Every thirty days the water level dropped a little over 1.5 meters, or 4 ft, until, by the beginning of August 1928, the prow of the first ship slipped above the surface. This was a moment of great excitement and national hubris, and thousands of politicians, tourists, academics and archeologists flocked to the lake to observe it. It was also, however, a moment of great anxiety, for as the first timbers began to emerge into the hot summer atmosphere, it was feared that they would immediately begin to dry out and disintegrate. The first priority therefore was to treat the timbers at the moment they emerged.

Relatively little was known at the time about the preservation of ancient, waterlogged timbers, but credit must be given to the presence of mind of early archeologists who ordered that the timbers be wrapped in waterlogged canvas as they came above the surface, pending more comprehensive treatment. Ultimately, upon the advice of Norwegian researchers who had successfully conserved several Viking ships excavated at the turn of the century, the timbers were stabilized using tar, linseed oil and turpentine before being treated with a resin solution.

By late September 1928, the first ship, named *prima nave*, lay entirely above water. Some two thirds of it, however, remained entombed in mud, and as soon as practical, a small army of workers set about the heavy work of digging it out. Archeologists then carefully cleared the residual mud from around the timbers, and wrapped them in damp canvas. As the hull was slowly exposed, a supporting framework was built around it to shore it up. The same procedure began on the second ship, the *seconda nave*, as it too began to appear above the waterline.

As mud was slowly removed, archeologists began to sift through it, unearthing a cornucopia of artifacts that gradually began to confirm the sheer magnitude of this archeological find. Not only were these ships vast and almost perfectly preserved, but they clearly had been built to the highest standards of comfort and opulence, and for some very specific purpose. Among the first objects to catch their attention where the now famous bronze post heads that adorned the decking, each individually crafted as a satyr, a fawn or a nymph. Likewise, the animal head moorings, and the bronze lion heads that capped the steering oar, and numerous, more enigmatic pieces that probably had ritual significance. An example of the latter would be the face of Medusa, also cast in bronze, or a pair of hands, left and right, which puzzled archeologists for some time. It was eventually determined that these were ritualistic, intended as a warning, or as protection against hostile spiritual powers. Scattered around the site, and contained in the rubble, where hundreds of bricks, sections of marble and numerous gilded copper tiles that would have adorned the corridors and colonnades. Smaller artifacts included coins, keys and fishhooks, as well as mosaic fragments of the highest artistic quality, including the two prevalent mosaic styles of the period, *opus tessellatum* and *opus sectile*, respectively cube-in-mortar and cut marble inlay styles.

Both ships emerged from the mud in a remarkable state of preservation, thanks largely to the fact that each had been encased in mud, which protected the timbers from degeneration and from the predations of early salvage attempts. Ultimately, some 31 million tons of water, or 1.4 billion cubic feet of water was pumped out of the lake, after which it took a further year to fully expose the first ship, and then carefully lift it free of the mud. The second ship did not begin to emerge until much later, and was not fully exposed and lifted until mid-1931. This ship, the *seconda nave*, slightly larger than the first, had been in deeper water, and so had been less accessible, and so less impacted by early salvage.

By October 1932, both ships had been successfully excavated and hauled up to shore, and placed under cover in a temporary hanger. At that point, archeologists and naval architects were at liberty to study and map both ships, and a series of detailed drawings were produced, which were largely archived and reproduced by Guido Ucelli in his book, *Le Navi di Nemi*. Obviously the sheer size of the two ships was the first matter of interest, but it became clear quite soon that both ships had been built along the lines of standard Roman ocean-going sail ships of the period, or Laburnum. Neither ship, however, had any means of practical propulsion, although the most obvious feature of the *seconda nave* was the outriggers sufficient to accommodate perhaps 100 oarsmen. Clearly, neither ship could have been effectively maneuvered on Lake Nemi, so both, no matter what their design specifics, had in essence been built as large houseboats of the most decadent sort, and most likely permanently fixed in position. Thanks to their extraordinary state of preservation, both wrecks offered a rare and perhaps unique opportunity for experts to study the techniques employed in the construction of a Roman shell-first, mortise-and-tenon ship of this size and weight.

While naval architects pored over the technicalities, archeologists pondered the historical significance of the ships. Once fully exposed, both ships were moved on a system of rails off the lakebed and into large temporary hangers constructed on the shore. It quickly became clear, however, that even this partial exposure to the elements, to fluctuating temperatures and humidity, was beginning to damage the timbers and surviving features of the superstructures. Local businessmen, merchants and suppliers, therefore, rallied to the cause and supplied the materials necessary for the construction of a custom museum on the north shore of the lake, the site believed to be the original shipyard.

The *Museo delle Navi Romane* was commissioned in 1932, and constructed between 1933 and 1939, becoming the first museum built specifically for what it was intended to exhibit. Two wings were included in the design to accommodate the ships, with further facilities to display selections of the enormous quantities of artifacts recovered. The facility was opened in 1936 by Mussolini himself.

Chapter 6: The Destruction of the Ships

Benito Mussolini's grandiose personal delusion was destined to suffer no less of a crushing defeat than that of Caligula. The same year that Mussolini inaugurated the *Museo delle Navi Romane*, he signed a treaty with Nazi Germany, creating what would be termed the *Axis Alliance*. At the stroke of a pen, Mussolini threw his lot in with German Chancellor Adolf Hitler, and by doing so committed Italy to war on the side of fascism.

Italian fortunes in the early part of the war were promising, with the Italian occupation of much of the Horn of Africa and Libya, and with bellicose Italian militancy dwarfing the Allied presence in Africa. In Europe, the Germans had successfully overrun Western Europe, and were threatening the British Isles in a coordinated air operation that they believed would see the Luftwaffe pound the British into defeat. In Africa, Mussolini was poised on the northern frontiers of the British Empire in Africa, confidently predicting that he would seize on behalf of the great Italian Empire the lion's share of colonial Africa.

The Italian military machine, however, proved itself as empty of substance as Mussolini himself. A series of catastrophic Italian and Axis reverses in the African theatre, combined with Hitler's ill-fated decision to open the Eastern Front, began a process of reverse in the Mediterranean theatre that would see the Germans retreating up the boot of Italy, and the Italians surrendering to the Allied advance on September 8, 1943. Mussolini himself was detained by Italian partisans and shot on April 25, 1945.

However, as the Allies pressed northwards up through Italy, pushing German forces back, the Germans systematically plundered the art and archeological heritage of Italy to the extent that it was possible for a retreating army to do so. Hitler and Goering had in particular competed with one another in the acquisition of looted European art, and what could not be crated up and carried away was quite often destroyed. The Allies became aware of the damage and losses being inflicted on the European artistic and architectural heritage, upon which, in 1943, the *Monuments, Fine Arts, and Archives* program was formed. The four hundred service members in the MFAA were mostly art historians and museum personnel who came to be known as *Monuments Men*.

In anticipation of the Allied invasion, Gen. Dwight Eisenhower issued a statement to the Allied Army during the summer of 1944, regarding the protection of art treasures: "Shortly we will be fighting our way across the continent of Europe in battles designed to preserve our civilization. Inevitably, in the path of our advance will be found historical monuments and cultural centers which symbolize to the world all that we are fighting to preserve. It is the responsibility of every commander to protect and respect these symbols whenever possible."

Inevitably, however, a number of important sites and monuments were damaged and destroyed during the fierce fighting that characterized the Italian Campaign. Perhaps one of the most highly publicized was the destruction of the ancient monastery at Monte Cassino early in 1944, but no less tragic was the blowing of the magnificent bridges of Florence.

The Ruins of Monte Cassino

From Monte Cassino, however, the Allies advanced slowly on Rome. On May 28, 1944, a German artillery position was established in the Alban Hills, within 400 ft of the *Museo delle Navi Romane*. By then Allied forces were pressing in on the Italian capital, and directly in the line of advance lay Lakes Nemi and Albano. The agitated German troops manning the artillery post began to come under allied fire, and as they prepared to retreat, they turned their attention to the museum. According to museum staff, the Germans began to vandalize the building before setting fire to the two preserved ships. The official report on the matter published in 1944, claimed that the episode was a willful act of destruction on the part of retreating German soldiers. A German press editorial, however, perhaps quoting the troops involved, or perhaps simply refuting enemy propaganda, blamed the event on incoming Allied artillery fire, and incendiary bombing.

The truth of how the Nemi ships met their destruction has been furiously debated, but since no definitive proof is available, the truth will probably never be known. The weight of evidence, however, would certainly suggest direct culpability on the part of those German troops present at the time. The natural areas and small settlements in the Alban hills would not have been a direct Allied target in relation to the advance on Rome, however, if the German artillery was actively bombarding advancing Allied columns, then it is not inconceivable that return artillery fire would have been registered very close to the museum. Some reports, indeed, state that the museum did register a direct hit. It has also been suggested that German troops set fire to the relics in order to delay advancing Allied troops, who it was assumed would attempt to extinguish the blaze.

The debate, however, is largely fruitless. German troops fled the scene, leaving behind the smoldering embers of the 2,000-year-old ships that had been available for study and observation for just 15-years. The ships were almost totally destroyed. While restoring the wreck of the museum was relatively easy, the loss of the main exhibits was incalculable. The vast chambers that once housed those great ships now stand virtually empty. A handful of artifacts – the stock anchor, the lead and ceramic cylinders and a handful of other miscellaneous items – accompany two scale models of the ship. The basement of the museum houses an archive of scorched timbers and thousands of nails among other sundry surviving fragments.

What did survive, however, were many of the bronze artifacts that had been transported and stored in Rome, and the detailed archeological site plans and technical drawings that had been drawn up and compiled by the Italian navy. Although these documents were collected and published in 1940 by Guido Ucelli, the loss of such a unique relic of ancient technology and construction can hardly be seen as anything less than catastrophic.

Chapter 7: Project Diana

The survival of these documents and drawings presented the opportunity for supporters and enthusiasts to contemplate an ambitious project to recreate at least one of the Nemi ships. In 1995, the *Association Dianae Lacus*, or the *Lake of Diana Association*, was founded to preserve the culture and history of the Lake Nemi area, with an emphasis on continuing the ongoing investigation and preservation of the site of Diana's Temple. Under the aegis of the *Association Dianae Lacus*, Project Diana was launched to take on the practical task of building the replica craft.

So far there has been some material commitment, and a certain amount of moral encouragement, but to date a replica keel has been produced and nothing more. No press releases have been made since 2004, and the *Dianae Lacus* web site was deleted on 1 October 2011.

Online Resources

Other books about Ancient Rome by Charles River Editors

Other books about the Nemi ships on Amazon

Bibliography

Ancient Works:

Cassius Dio, *Roman History*, Book 59

Josephus, *Antiquities of the Jews*, Books XVIII–XIX

Philo of Alexandria, *On the Embassy to Gaius*

Seneca the Younger

Suetonius, *The Lives of Twelve Caesars*, Life of Caligula

Modern Works:

Balsdon, V. D. (1934). *The Emperor Gaius.*

Barrett, Anthony A. (1989). *Caligula: the corruption of power.*

Grant, Michael (1979). *The Twelve Caesars.*

Hurley, Donna W. (1993). *An Historical and Historiographical Commentary on Suetonius' Life of C. Caligula.*

Printed in Great Britain
by Amazon

36285047R00020